William Joy Parker

Minimalism

from a different point of view.
What are the pros and cons of living a minimalist lifestyle?

What are the downsides of minimalism?

Furthermore, the transmission, duplication or reproduction of any of the following work, including precise information, will be considered an illegal act, irrespective whether it is done electronically or in print. The legality extends to creating a secondary or tertiary copy of the work or a recorded copy and is only allowed with express written consent of the Publisher. All additional rights are reserved.

The information in the following pages is broadly considered to be a truthful and accurate account of facts, and as such any inattention, use or misuse of the information in question by the reader will render any resulting actions solely under their purview. There are no scenarios in which the publisher or the original author of this work can be in any fashion deemed liable for any hardship or damages that may befall them after undertaking information described herein.

Additionally, the information found on the following pages is intended for informational purposes only and should thus be considered, universal. As befitting its nature, the information presented is without assurance regarding its continued validity or interim quality. Trademarks that mentioned are done without written consent and can in no way be considered an endorsement from the trademark holder.

Contents

Introduction: Not Just Another "Minimalism" Guide

"Simplicity, clarity, singleness: These are the attributes that give our lives power and vividness and joy as they are also the marks of great art." ~Richard Holloway

Minimalism is a lifestyle philosophy that places experiences and personal well-being above the materials things cluttering up your life. It is designed to simplify every aspect of life from your closet to your obligations. Minimalism is designed to make you think about how many relationships, acquaintances, and friends you can take care of at one time. It is streamlining your life and maintaining a low impact on the world. You only own what you need to survive, and you avoid spending money on replacing or maintaining items. Minimalism advocates simplicity, even if this means taking income and a prosperous future out of the picture.

According to dictionary theories, minimalism "removes the meaningless to make room for the meaningful." Minimalism means living with only the things you need. Having only a few possessions is a popular concept and leads one to avoid the stress caused by trying to out-do your neighbors and friends. With minimalism, you have a clarity of mind that you are living a fulfilled life. Minimalism's philosophy is a great precept if taken in the right spirit.

Minimalist bloggers remind us daily that plainness is not a religion, it is a great approach to simplicity, but it is not the answer to every problem. Minimalist lifestyles can have legitimate motivations, but sanctimonious anti-consumerism of the dogmatic minimalist isn't a motivation. Showing off how little you have is counterproductive; you are cluttering your mind and emotions with "I am better than you" attitudes that come from decluttering your possessions and living sparingly.

Austereness is a trending style that is also popular in music, art, and design. In the arts, minimalism emphasizes extreme simplification of form and the use of monochromatic pallets of primary colors and basic shapes. You can also ascribe minimalism to music or a reductive style that uses only simple rhythms, patterns, and simple sonorities. To put it simply, minimalism is characterized by extreme sparseness and simplicity. If you are a minimalist, you are one who favors restrictions and often sets goals to a minimum.

Difference between Minimalism and Simple Living

Although the two terms, minimalism and simple living, seem to be interchangeable, there is a noticeable difference between the two topics. Minimalism is a catchall phrase for those who are attracted to externally paring down to the minimums in their life. Phrases and single words often used by minimalists to describe their lifestyle are austerities, de-cluttering, anti-consumerism, getting rid of stuff, and eliminating as much as possible. When thinking about minimalism discipline becomes a watchword. There is nothing wrong with those terms, but it does make one want to stop and think about lifestyles.

Extreme minimalism seems to attract those who are young and male. This class of people tend to be able to work through thoughts and emotions with a sense of purpose. Women who are often fascinated by minimalism are those who are aware that a lifestyle of minimalism is practical in this age of overconsumption. Women have specific items they love for comfort, and they often surround themselves with the stuff that provides emotional release.

Simple living embraces life much more gently and internally than does minimalism. A simple life means integrating uncomplicatedness in every area of your life. Living simply does not focus on total stuff elimination, making lists and de-cluttering, simple living is identifying the things that add value and joy to your life. Simplicity means freedom to be yourself, natural, living authentically, and caring for the environment. Simple living is contentment.

Those who love simple living appear to be experienced, concerned with family, and established. After you have worked and lived for years and been a part of the consumption and consumer lifestyle, there is an awareness of how much you to turn to a simpler life.

Simple living is more of a family or community approach. It is not, however living in a commune, and gardening for the rest of your life while sleeping in a monk's corner. It is finding a way to continue learning, doing things you love, and finding

The differences between simple living and minimalism are not black and white. Minimalism and simple living do complement and strengthen each other and can be considered as two parts of a whole. As you move through your life's journey, you may find that both minimalism and simplicity will evolve into something totally different. Think about smart living and practicality. Live simple and involve some of the traits of minimalism. Be a consumer, but be smart (Gottberg, 2015).

Types of Minimalist

There are different definitions of what minimalism is. Reading through these different types of minimalists, you may find yourself reflecting a certain minimalist type. Don't panic; it's all good.

The creative minimalist is resourceful and artsy. They feel that minimalism is a way to express themselves. They are found looking through other people's trash and turning it into art, donating stuff to thrift stores, and their homes are very minimal. The furniture they use has been repurposed, rebuilt and refinished. They love simple art; pieces that emphasize primary colors.

The traveling minimalist is a bit on the extreme side. They are usually outgoing and adventurous. They often have a smile on their face, and a mission in their heart. They usually own less than 100 items and live out of a duffel bag. You can recognize a traveling minimalist by the worn out shoes they wear and a sweatshirt tied around their waist. A traveling minimalist may also live in a tent. They cook outside and carry all their possessions. They are usually nature lovers and spend very little time with attachments, relationships, or emotional entanglements.

There are minimalists who are intentionally homeless. They seem somewhat happy with their lifestyle and are free of attachments, stuff, and responsibility. They have to worry about a bed and board but carry out their lives by being a super-tramp to staying exclusively in hostels. Some intentionally homeless minimalists are even business men. There is a consultant who works in a New York firm who is intentionally homeless and prides himself because he only owns 15 items. He does make a nice living however and hoards his money in his backpack.

The next time you see someone on the street with their belonging in a grocery cart, you might want to ask them if they love their minimalist life. You will probably find out that they would rather have a nice home and stuff in one place.

The tiny house minimalist is an off-shoot minimalist movement gaining popularity. Living quarters are set on someone else's lawn, a small bit of land, or living quarters can be mobile. These homes are so tiny that they require no planning permission, no mortgage and have little overhead. These homeowners might have electricity and hot water, but very little else. You can find these minimalists and their tiny houses on country parcels. Google "tiny houses" to see examples of tiny house minimalists.

The accidental minimalist is one who became a minimalist by force rather than choice. This type of minimalist may have lost their job, become divorced, have no family or friends, and have no options left, but simplicity and minimalism. They may be homeless or living very sparsely in a small apartment.

An accidental minimalist might also be someone who is just tired of stuff. They stand in rooms they don't use and look at all the stuff around them. They stub their toes on stuff and finally decide enough is enough.

A professional minimalist is difficult to live around. These are the working professionals who have lofty goals to simplify their lives. They are the ones who have attitudes of superiority towards those who have stuff. Often a professional minimalist is driven to declutter to prove a point. They sometimes turn to the homes of their friends to try out their de-cluttering ideas. This attitude can lead to having few friends. Professional minimalists claim they are getting ready to travel, but they never seem to leave.

The original minimalist has always been a minimalist. They love their simple lifestyle and can almost be called an urban minimalist. They are down to earth, loving, grow their own food, and sit on their porch in a rocking chair contemplating the universe, or perhaps trying to determine the next thought to clear from their minds.

The curious minimalist is not really a minimalist by definition. They want a simpler lifestyle and they may dabble in simplifying. They have a simpler lifestyle, but are not really ready to scale down too much. They love their stuff and do want to become organized, but they only talk the talk instead of walking the walk (Sanger, 2014).

The small holdings minimalist lives in an eco-community and escapes to the country. They live very simply and farm the land only for what they need. They do not ask for much and work hard for basic comforts. These minimalists embrace a lifestyle that is built around sustainable practices. Often these are carefully planned neighborhoods that reflect simplicity and efficiency. It is a simple life and sometimes not all that comfortable.

If you have ever been to a huge and highly populated city, you will note that there are many people living in very small places. They intentionally live in the attics of larger homes or apartment houses that have minimal corner rooms. Most of these minimalists' homes have unique architecture designed to maximize the space. These minimalists, who choose to live in these miniscule flats over larger homes, love their small spaces. The overhead is less expensive;

they enjoy simple spaces, and their lives can be very sparse, but unique.

Dogmatic minimalism is similar to a professional minimalist. They own only 100 items or less. If they own a car at all, it is older and barely runs. They urge you to get rid of your television and live a life of meditation. Reading is a great pastime and this type of minimalist believes in reading self-help books. Dogmatic minimalism states you should not any type of distraction. If you have books keep the organized and in set places. Dogmatic minimalist demands an uncluttered home and mind. Dogmatic minimalists do not have many treasures, but they do have experiences to share.

Dogmatic minimalism can be a dramatic lifestyle change. An extremely good minimalist has no clutter and confusion in their thoughts or actions and details are never offered. They tend to answer questions with one-word answers.

What do extreme or dogmatic minimalists do when they want to cook meals at home or need a tool to fix a door? They typically borrow items they don't have.

They often share living space with others and generally have very simple eating habits. That's all well and good, but if they need to borrow to exist, then aren't they really being irresponsible and bothersome?

A practical minimalist is one who doesn't have to count stuff. You just subscribe to minimalism as a practical means to a simple, but comfortable existence. You don't believe it is a good idea to throw out all of your stuff immediately. You let others live their life of commercialism, and you join them in their buying sprees at times. You make the transition to being a "real" minimalist at your own pace and in your own time. In the meantime, you enjoy your stuff.

Minimalists are proud of their trendy progress. They tend to bring their friends and family into their homes and proudly show how little they have. What little they have includes the clothes their closet, cupboards, and seating arrangements. They often act self-congratulatory and obnoxious. Being a minimalist does not make you a better person.

There is more to minimalism than just de-cluttering things and throwing out the physical stuff. Minimalism demands that you clear out unused and irrelevant thoughts in your mind. Take away emotions that get in the way of simplicity. Those who embrace minimalism state that in its purest form minimalism is "the intentional promotion of the things we most value and the removal of everything that distracts from it." Minimalism forces change. (Becker, 2015). A big question asked by those who do not understand minimalism, how do you determine what is most valuable physically and emotionally? How do you determine what is important?

To answer that question, minimalism seeks to bring freedom from the overwhelming passion to possess things. It stops consumerism in your life and forces you to seek happiness inside yourself. The value of relationships, experiences and taking care of your soul is at the heart of minimalism and the center of living a good life.

Simplify your life and become a minimalist by contemplating these ideas, but beware of being too caught up in your minimalist lifestyle changes that you lose focus on what is important to you.

Too many material possessions complicate lives. They drain your bank account, energy, and attention. Possessions keep you from the ones you love and prevent you living a life based on values.

Your lives are too filled with time commitments. If possible release yourself from time commitments that do not line up with your values.

Reduce your goals. Reducing your totals down to two or three major wishes should improve your focus and success rate. Use the list tactic to write down what you want to accomplish in your life.

Negative emotions are useless. Get rid of resentment, hate, and jealousy. Smile all the time and take responsibility for the thoughts going through your mind.

Reduce your debt. Do what you can do to get out from under the weight of debt. Sacrifice luxury and duplicate items.

Use fewer words. Keep your speech plain and definitely avoid gossip and lengthy explanations. Mumble when needed.

Avoid artificial ingredients in your diet. Reduce your consumption of over-the-counter medicines. Let your body heal on its own.

Get rid of constant distractions. That means all your electronic devices.

Stop multi-tasking. It reduces productivity. Do one thing at a time, but do it well.

It is true that consumers are all too hurried, too rushed, and too stressed. You work long hours to pay bills and gain more possessions. People blast from one activity to another, multitasking along the way and never seeming to get anything done. Most of you are in constant connection with your jobs and others via cell phones. You have no real relationships; only electronic friends.

Will simplifying and getting rid of your possessions make you less stressed? Or is it a Catch-22 position? Would you rather have nothing to do and deny your children, friends and family the opportunities to choose for themselves? Should you continue your consuming ways and be a very busy, but contributing person?

Minimalism can be great if you go about it the right way. Note that stuff does not really go away. For example, if you declutter your desktop with a new computer and move your files, CDs and all your books plus your paperwork to the computer, you have not created a simpler lifestyle. You have just moved things around. (Most people will save their CDs and DVDs in storage boxes in case they need to

Paring down your clothes to the point they all fit on one rail is great, but what happens if you have given away a piece of clothing that you need? Do you go out and purchase another item that is just like the one you just discarded or do you feel cheated and stressed because you no longer have the items you need?

Becoming a Minimalist?

It is not easy to embrace a minimalist lifestyle. Even though removing the meaningless details and possessions in your life to make room for the significant can be very appealing. You load up your excess possessions and drop items at the Goodwill. Everything you think is excessive and non-essential you sell on Craig's List or eBay. Now you have few possessions, and you wonder, "Now what? Was there a point to this de-cluttering?" You stand in the middle of your barren room and shake your head.

Removing the physical excess is an important part of minimalism, and to many they believe the major goal is to get rid of material possessions. However, let minimalism be the tool that takes you beyond your possessions and gives you the determination to make room for the most important intangibles of experiences, emotions, and time. Sounds incredibly wonderful doesn't it?

Minimalism is essentially an instrument to help you find freedom from worry, fear, overwhelming responsibility, and guilt. You no longer have multiple possessions to take care of and worry over. You are free from the depression of the trappings of a consumer culture in your life. Stress is gone, and you smile all the time and wonder why your family and friends find you a bit strange.

After all is said and done, becoming a minimalist just sounds tiring. Getting rid of all your possessions, governing your thoughts and avoiding gossip is awesome when talked about, but in the end are you really going to get rid of the lifestyle you now live?

Getting Rid of Thoughts

Minimalism is getting rid of thoughts that are destructive. Live a simpler life and create more space in your mind and forget those feelings that cloud up your vision. Apply the same principles to uncluttering your mind as you used to unclutter your living space.

Begin by realizing positive thoughts and a negative thoughts cannot occupy the same space in your mind. Two opposite thoughts cannot co-exist together, or there will be confusion. Begin to choose thoughts that have meaning and value. Get rid of the thoughts that cause you remorse, stress, and unhappiness.

Move out of your brain space worries, fears, bad memories, questions, yearnings, and more "stuff." Just like your physical space you are going to clean out your mind, and move to a clean and open space.

Carefully choose what thoughts you are taking with you. Take only those thoughts that you plan to use in your minimalist life. Use the memories that are good and thoughts that are positive.

Find a place for everything you want to keep. Your thoughts have to occupy a space and remember no two thoughts can occupy the same space at the same time.

Apply the rule to live clutter free. Apply this to your mind. Positive thinking is the goal and decluttering your mind is the tool. You have the choice to take either a good memory or a worry, fear or courage, denial or acceptance. Choose wisely.

Trying to declutter your mind is a process. It takes adjustment, but it works if you sincerely let it (Becker, 2015).

Awesome words of wisdom, but very difficult to follow. Most thoughts are chaotic and jump from "room to room." If you can control your thoughts to follow minimalist ideals, you are amazing.

"Thoughts can be your worst friends", states Buddhist Monk Matthieu Ricard, "and your worst enemies." You mind has a path of its own and taking control of your thoughts and emotions to become less stressed and better equipped to solve problems is the goal of minimalism and decluttering your life.

When purging thoughts from your mind, pause where you are at, and take a deep breath. Literally tell yourself to stop thinking chaotic thoughts and focus on breathing. It takes 90 seconds of neurochemical triggers to fade from your brain and return you to happier thoughts.

Remain in the moment. Constantly thinking about the past and believing that you have no power to change your distressing thoughts will make things worse. Live in the moment. Thinking about right now will help to promote inner peace and clarity.

Think without judgement. Stick to objective, concrete facts and get rid of quality thoughts that could cause problems. Write down your thoughts and read them back to yourself.

Take action to address your thoughts. Develop a plan to address your thoughts and worries. Make a plan to separate your anxious thoughts from your happy thoughts. Remember that two thoughts cannot live in the same space.

Place yourself in a comfortable environment as you de-clutter your mind. The outside world affects your inner world. If you are in a place where you feel uncomfortable or out of control, then move to somewhere where you are happier.

Unclutter your thoughts by doing another activity. Go for a run, watch a movie or talk to your significant others. Let them help you move thoughts out of your mind and into another place.

Above all, if you are trying to de-clutter your thoughts, do not try and choose your thoughts. Control them as they come into your mind. Think about controlling and moving your thoughts as they arrive rather than repressing them.

Chapter I: Why is Minimalism so Popular?

"The movement is growing ... almost every day." ~ Joshua Becker

The essence of minimalism is detachment. Detachment from physical stuff, ideas, thoughts and damaging emotions. It is not about having less or decluttering or even downsizing. These are the results of minimalism but are not the heart of it. To understand more about what minimalism is, look to the internet or your local bookstore.

New books, blogs, and forums are appearing almost every day concerning simplistic and minimalist living. More and more people are attracted to the lifestyle and adopting certain principles of a minimalist lifestyle. Why minimalism is growing so popular can be summarized in these ten different reasons:

Worldwide financial turmoil includes rising

unemployment low wages and falling stock prices. These problems are bringing families and individuals to the realization that they need to evaluate what possessions they hold and what items they need to purchase. Tighter budgets are the result of worldwide financial chaos and families are seeking ways to cut their budgets and expenditures. They sell their excess goods to have money for primary existence.

Environmental concerns are part of the minimalist life. Using less equals less of earth's natural resources being destroyed. More and more people are standing up for the right of the environment to remain viable and breathing. Commercialism means digging into the earth for resources to make useless goods. The earth is being destroyed because of commercialism.

People are becoming less impressed by the new things your friends have. Since you can't afford them, you tend to claim that you don't want them. You quickly develop the habit of not caring what others have, and you let them know that you do not care.

Personal debt or living beyond your means brings you to the realization that you need to stop purchasing "stuff" on credit. Debt is definitely a growing trend. Listen to Dave Ramsey, he advocates a cash based rather than a credit based life. An awesome thought, but what does it have to do with minimalism? You just spend cash rather than plastic for the things you want.

Minimalism needs to convince people that buying less is a worthwhile trend. Think about what you need before you make that next purchase. Consider, is it a want or a need?

The realization that there is more to life than just possessions. Consumerism is alive and well, and advertisers continue to bring new and better products to the market claiming each item is a step towards fulfillment and happiness. There is a growing trend of people, however, who are tired of trying to "keep up with the Jones'" and are finding happiness through relationships, social causes, and life's significance.

Technology is making the world smaller and bringing on a desire to live a simpler life. People turn to minimalism as they realize the poverty in the world. The question is, are you really giving away your excess to those in poverty? Is the money you saved by becoming a minimalist money helping these people live better lives? One can only hope.

Personal computing advances make minimalism easier to live than ever before. Computers have replaced the need for paper files, photo albums, calendars, and calculators. Computers, smartphones, and tablets have taken away books, phone books, magazines, and newspapers. Paper no longer clutters up your counter tops and furniture. How sad that the feel of tangible paper books and magazines is going away. If you love paper, you might have to go to the public library.

Minimalists can indoctrinate more and more people to their lifestyle via electronic and internet social media. Extreme minimalists make the lifestyle sound almost like nirvana; a happy place; and an exceptional existence. Just Google the word "minimalism" and you will find millions of articles on how to live simpler. It almost gets confusing.

Consumerism is still alive and well. Advertisers tell us that we need the next and best purchase, and this will bring us satisfaction. There is a growing trend of people who are seeing through the advertising hype and challenging this climate. They want to be different and get rid of possessions that are not making them happy. Minimalism is well and good, but what if you want a particular item? Will your minimalist conscience make you feel guilty, cause stress, and eventually bring on a nervous breakdown if you choose to acquire this item? Something to ponder.

Is Minimalism for You?

As noted in a previous chapter, simplicity and minimalism are different sides of the same coin. It is good to realize that minimalism is not the equivalent of living in a cave and eating berries by a fire, but it is a lifestyle when lived in moderation that can be helpful. Simple living is gentle and resourceful. It is not getting rid of clutter for de-cluttering's sake, simple living is real and internal.

Do you have stuff that you rarely use? Unnecessary clutter sends negative impacts on your life. Box up your duplicates and unused stuff. Be simple.

Do you have excessive debt? Try not purchasing more stuff until you have reduced your debt. Getting out of debt is practicality.

Do you long to own a nicer car, house or other stuff? If your car always breaks down, or you are envious of the neighbors, you need to sit back and think about where you are going. Materialism is the name of this "disease."

Are you busy, but your life lacks meaning? Everyone has days filled with activity and can end with feelings of emptiness. You might want to look into minimalism to remove excess to make room for meaningful activates. Pare down and live simply.

These realizations do not necessarily mean you are ready to become a minimalist, but that you are human and concerned with your lifestyle. Perhaps you do need to declutter and make your life simpler. You can organize and declutter your life without subscribing to the minimalist philosophy that demands you live with less.

House, Car, Cellphone and Jewelry

If you want to learn to detach yourself from your stuff, try this technique. Think of one item in your life that you love. It might be your car or computer, your television, or your wardrobe. Take that item and break it down to its core purpose. Your car is for transportation, the television is for entertainment, and clothes are for wearing. Think about the downsides of your one item. Your car is expensive, your television encourages laziness, and your clothes make

Consider what your life would be like if you don't possess that expensive item. Would your life be noticeably different? Write down the item, think about it, and draw a picture of how you would be without that item. If you are truly dedicated to a minimalist lifestyle, you will draw a picture of you being happy. If you have no desire to minimize, then draw a picture of you being sad. At this point, don't get rid of your stuff. There is no reason to be sad over getting rid of your possessions.

In today's modern culture, it is emphasized that the good life is found in possessions – and as many as possible. Happiness is shopping at the mall and filling your home with useless, but awesome accessories. To some people, this is the ultimate happiness. The joy of finding a bargain or just something that makes you giddy is happiness. There is absolutely nothing wrong with this type of lifestyle. Do not let your minimalist friends thumb their noses at you as you ride off on your ATV's, camper or boat. You are making memories with your stuff, and that is the best thing in the world.

Commercialism and materialism are the driving force behind manufacturing, jobs, and the economy. The stuff that comes from productivity is the stuff of dreams. Keep dreaming and consuming.

Minimalism as a Tool for Happiness

Minimalism should be used as a tool or a guide to a happier and simpler life, but it can be harmful to you, your family, your ambition, and your business. Minimalism is the emerging philosophy of having less physically, emotionally and intellectually. "Freeing yourself from commercialism and getting rid of passions and the drive to work hard, will lead you to becoming supremely happy," so claims proponents of minimalism.

Minimalism is a trend. It is today's "less is more" mantra. The days of opulence and semi-opulence in fashion, homes styles and arts are no longer in vogue. Minimalism in makeup, naked eyes, and hair that looks slept in, and clothing that is comfortable, interchangeable, and wrinkled is the new modern. Minimalism is clean lines, shoes and dresses with no fluff. It is a color palette that subscribes mainly to neutrals. It is the inclination is to develop a capsule wardrobe and pare down stuffed closets.

Minimalism is trying to live a more intentional life. By

focusing less on the material goods, there is more time to focus on the meaningful – experiences, travel, play time, and relaxation. Possessions, so it is said, weigh you down. When you have less clutter in your life, you have room for experiences. Forget purchasing that handbag, use the money for something else that will bring interest to your life. Break away from your job and head off to the mountains; you can finish projects later or better yet find a new job. Sub-lease your apartment, rent out your home. There is nothing in your home or apartment that anyone can steal or break. You have gotten rid of everything. By not purchasing stuff on credit, your credit card limit is high and you can take off on a road trip. Run up the credit card gathering experiences and memories. Take off on a road trip. By having less; you live more.

Seems a bit of an oxymoron. How do you get these fun pleasures if you have a laisse faire attitude about your job and just take off whenever you want? Sounds delightful and highly irresponsible. Spontaneity is wonderful, but the business world and the economy does not work in that manner. Most people need to plan, save and be responsible.

Minimalists use this philosophy to justify becoming obsessed with hunting down every double or unneeded object in their home. They go from room to room looking for items that are unnecessary. Items are swept out from under family members, roommates and users by the minimalist saying, "You don't need this." Minimalists continually deny themselves and become crazy in their new found philosophy of "less is more." They urge everyone they meet to become as obsessed as they are.

Minimalism is not the goal. It should be a tool to learn how to declutter, organize, and clean-up. The true minimalist has learned how to push down emotions that came on when you throw out items that are keepsakes. One young man was cleaning out his home on his trip to becoming a minimalist and threw his grandmother's Japanese vase from WWII in the trash. It was found by an antique dealer who valued the vase at $10,000.

If you regret tossing out your stuff, minimalists say, "so what, tamp down the emotions." Your decluttering is a way to happiness, and your spending ban is leading you to nirvana. If you lost valuable items in your frenzy to clean out your home, it doesn't matter. Your clutter is gone, and you are happy.

Is it Popular to be Happy through Minimalism?

Happiness is thought of as the good life and freedom from suffering. It is flourishing, having joy, prosperity, well-being, and contentment. It is the pursuit of trying to find what makes us happy. Researchers have made the study of happiness an entire sub-culture. There is still little definitive definitions about happiness. Defining happiness is elusive, but psychologists say that it is necessary to study strengths and what makes us happy. By better understanding human tendencies we can learn how to prevent disorders, learn to become happier, and develop the ultimate lifestyle for happiness.

Happiness is intangible. If you want to be happy, you must learn to thrive in whatever lifestyle you choose. Strengths, positive emotions, and resilience equal happiness. The more we understand what makes us happy, the better we can understand the need to live a simple life of minimalism or a life full of possessions and stuff.

A study conducted in the 1970s attempted to determine the level of happiness in people who thought their lives were perfect. Psychologists discovered that those who had won lotteries and had tons of money were no happier those who just meet their basic needs. It was determined that money and possessions can buy short term happiness. Social experts also state that once you have a level of happiness due to financial gain, you are now in a materialistic cycle. You try stay happy through the constant purchase material items.

This cycle may be true for some but there are also countless other people who have good jobs, high incomes, possessions, and know when their belongings make them happy. A nice home, good car, money to travel, and giving their family advantages can make them happy. Do they strive for more? Possibly, but that striving for more makes them happy.

This same study discovered that participants who spend money on others experienced great happiness. They had feelings of euphoria, contentment, and altruism. Money made them happy; possessions were awesome.

Minimalists who have little money to spend on others, tend to be on the selfish side. They are thinking only about their minimalist lifestyle, their own well-being, and achieving simplicity in their lives. They may physically help others, but giving material wealth is out of the question.   Trying to determine what lifestyle will bring you the most happiness can leave you in a very interesting situation. Do I declutter and give everything away, or do I work hard, earn money, and help others with my wealth? What will give me the greatest sense of happiness?

What will lead to happiness and fulfillment?

Vilfredo Pareto, an Italian economist, stated that 80% of happiness comes from 20% of lifestyle activities. To follow Pareto's experiment, pinpoint what brings you fulfillment and happiness. Maximize your time and resources to that 20%. Break down what makes you happy and follow what lifestyle makes you happiest.

Martin Luther King, Jr. wrote that we need to find a way to become motivated to make a difference. Is minimalism this answer or can you help others with the possessions you have. One extraordinary family built a large cabin. They filled it with all the things they loved and enjoyed. Their philosophy? We will allow others to use this cabin and enjoy our possessions. We open up our home to underprivileged children, friends who need a place to "get away from it all", and those who cannot afford to have an experience in a cabin. Getting rid of their possessions would not give this family the opportunity to serve others.

"You are unique because of your individual traits, skills, experiences, aptitudes, interests and attitudes. You are not the sum of your possessions, but those possessions can give you joy if you share them with others" (Jolibois, 2015).

Wealth does not necessarily provide any guarantee of a good life. What matters is how you spend it. Giving money away might make you happier than just spending it on yourself. If you have money and possessions, you are happier when you use them for experiences. If you are a minimalist, you do not have the financial ability to provide different and happy experiences. It is awesome to walk through the park or breathe in nature, but what if your happiness is having a Minecraft tournament, or a swimming expedition, or even a trip to a sunny island. How can you live and enjoy extraordinary experiences without planning, saving, and involving stuff? Studies over the past ten years have shown that life experiences do give us lasting pleasure, but many people believe that material possessions offer better value than simple experiences. Happenings without props are fleeting. Material goods last longer and provide meaningful experiences and emotions. You can provide significant experiences if you have possessions to share and enjoy. On a camping trip last summer, a neighbor cleaned out their garage and found old inner tubes. They had the tubes repaired, filled with air and took them on their camping expedition to the river. Three little boys had the time of their life tubing down the river, racing and splashing one another and eating steaks around the campfire after their river experience. What experience would they have had if the inner tubes had been de-cluttered from the garage and their father said, "Hey we don't need these old inner tubes. Let's get rid of them in the landfill." The trick is not to live for your possessions. Use them to make you happy, but also foster appreciation and gratitude for what you have. You can be equally happy as a consumer by using and taking care of your possessions. Keep a daily journal of happy experiences and express your gratitude. Minimalism does not guarantee that you will maintain this attitude. Minimalism could, in fact, make you angry, unsatisfied, and very unhappy.

Chapter II: Minimalism Is a Double-edged Sword

"Minimalism is downright harmful to you, your ambition and our business." ~ Peter Shallard

Pundits state that minimalism is more than living with less and radically reducing the amount of things you purchase and own. It is freeing you from modern "keeping up with the Jones'" attitude, and continually trying to acquire more than you can possibly use. Freeing yourself from possessions comes down to living from a cardboard box, or a home with little in the way of décor. Your life is seeking experiences over objects.

Minimalism is looking for that elusive feel-good anti-commercialism vibe. However, as you dig deeper into minimalism, the philosophy can become dangerous and destructive. Seeking to have less is a reverse snobbery attitude that can ruin your relationships, family life, and if you are a business owner, it can ruin your business.

Minimalism is Toxic to Businesses

The minimalistic philosophy specifies that you get rid of stuff that cause clutter, stress, and distress. Perhaps you believe your marketing program needs revamping and de-cluttering. You begin to skimp on marketing. You don't bring in customers, and you can't earn the profits you need to stay in businesses. Minimizing on what you think are useless marketing strategies will put your business in the red.

When employing minimalist tactics to your business, maybe you should get rid of those perks that lift up employee morale. These perks are expensive and take away from the simplicity of your company. Your employees quickly lose their job satisfaction and loss of job satisfaction will break your business. Low morale and loss of perks can translate into reduced productivity, higher health care costs, and high turnover. But you have lower employee costs and your business looks much more streamlined. Minimalist business practices mean you might operate unethically to streamline your inventory. You no longer go into work as often, and you begin selling expired products, refuse to update, and stop carrying enough inventory. You do other unacceptable things that will tarnish your company's reputation. All streamlining and de-cluttering are in the name of minimalism.

You begin to become very lazy, and this is one of the worst habits you can develop. Laziness affects motivation and your willingness to meet deadlines. Productivity suffers, and you are not able to meet clients' demands. In fact, you don't care. You feel your clients are too materialistic, and they need to adopt a minimalist attitude.

You do not take the risks that you need to move your company beyond your competition.

As a minimalist, you refuse to reinvest. You keep the profits you have made and hoard them. You do not reinvest in your organization; you do not fix what is broken, and you let vital equipment fall into disrepair. An unsuccessful business is what can happen if you try and employ minimalist tactics to your business.

Minimalism can be Lethal to Your Relationships

If you are determined to be a minimalist, you need to invest time in certain relationships. Determine who is worthy of your time, and who you consider to be lethal. The entire precept of minimalism is to de-clutter your life including your mind, relationships, and emotions. Minimalists say that the process of becoming spare requires a change in perceptive and determining what people contribute to you quality of life.

When considering minimalism and relationships you need to determine how to be generous and kind to others but at the same time distance yourself from those you don't want to be a big part of your life. It is easy to develop a connection with a coworker or roommate or someone who is always there, but these may not be the people who had value to your life. Everyone has had a "friend" or someone who doesn't deserve to be in your lives. They drain us of emotion, and are high maintenance. There is always someone in your life who isn't supportive and who takes and takes without giving back to the relationship. Those who contribute very little and prevent you from growing needs to be decluttered from your lives. In the world of minimalism people and relationships are the most important part of the plan. If minimalism does not help the relationships and causes more harm than good, it needs to be used in a different way. When developing a minimalist attitude and need to decrease the tensions try these simple ways: Change yourself first. Be positive and focus on things that you are yours fist. Forget their stuff or stuff that is both of yours.

Explain your way of thinking. Discuss how it will benefit your relationship. For example, "When I get rid of all my computer games I will have many extra hours just for us. Might work if you are a game-aholic!

Time changes people in different ways. Let the other person take the time they need to be okay with getting rid of their stuff.

Make it a team effort. If you are trying to minimize an entire family, it needs to be a team effort.

If your relationship or friendship is suffering because of your minimalist attitude, the relationship should win.

If acquaintances react negatively to your new lifestyle, then they can be de-cluttered from your life.

Try to explain your reasoning in a very clear and concise manner. List out the pros and cons of your new lifestyle. Chances are others are considering the same lifestyle or live a minimalist life and you don't even know it.

Owning Stuff

Minimalism claims that you must own less stuff. Sounds good, but why do you own stuff in the first place? Owning stuff is awesome. From the beginning of time, people have sought to own stuff – tools, fire, animal skins for clothing, etc. It is a natural tendency to create better tools for living. Where would we be without our ancestors seeking to own stuff? "This means we've all evolved from the proto-consumers who had the best tools.

Our ancestors loved their stuff!" (Shallard, 2015). Ask yourself, "would you be comfortable living in a home without stuff?"

Getting rid of stuff has its advantages, and minimalism stresses that there are three areas that will profit from getting rid of stuff:

Environment.

By reducing consumer habits, there will be less impact on the planet's resources. Man's footprint will be reduced by you buying less, manufacturers making less, valuable resources being left in the ground, and poverty increasing. To provide the environment that minimalist long to promote, consumerism seeks to find new ways to keep the environment clean while developing materials and efficient energy. People are not going to cut down on owning stuff, and there will always be demands on the environment. The key is conservation and finding ways to safely dispose of waste. Minimalism by its very philosophy demands you declutter which adds to the landfills.

Financial.

If you consume less, you don't need as much money. You won't need to work as hard earning money and will have time for other pleasures. You won't however, have the money for movies, quality food, and travel. The economy depends on the law of supply and demand. When consumer demand is high and corporations produce huge quantities of products, jobs are created and the economy flourishes. Not purchasing products can have a devastating effect on the economy. Without goods to purchase people be unable to purchase goods, have choices, pay their rent, or buy food. Seeking more and trying to live a commercial life keeps the economy growing. Perhaps if consumers had adopted a minimalist mindset decades ago, the economy would be in a less wasteful shape, and there would be no need to de-clutter lives. Learning, working, innovating, and wisely using the earth's resources gives us the opportunity to learn more, to create, and to explore. Minimalism equals stagnate learning and stifling creativity.

Aesthetic.

Reducing physical possessions will provide you with a clean and manageable living space. You can clean your home in under an hour. Now, what do you do? Where are you going to dispose of your unwanted possessions? Decluttering equals landfills that are environmentally poor options. You load up your garbage can with unwanted items, take them to the curb, wait for garbage day and watch your excess stuff head off to the landfill. Minimalism also claims that its purpose is not to dispose of beautiful or user things. Minimalism supposedly prompts you to determine what is of value and what isn't. It urges you to get rid of those things that are useless in your life. Where do these unwanted items go? To the Goodwill so others can use them, to the landfill to get them out of the way, or to the incinerator to cause more air pollution.

Minimalists state, "If something is available in a shop, it has been 'permitted' and is therefore unlikely to be worth owning. Subscribing to libraries and tinkering with free hobbies make us rich. Owning things makes us financially, spatially, intellectually and spiritually poor" (Wringham, 2015). What a scary premise. Are we all spiritually poor because there is consumption, hoarding, purchasing, and re-consuming?

Commercialism

Commercialism is the manufacturing and consumption of "stuff" that is geared toward personal usage, methods, aims and free enterprise. It is intended to generate profits. Materialism and commercialism to some people are the successes and progress you achieve; the highest values in your life. Minimalists claim that commercialism is a question of belief. It is a simple idea that focuses on material things as opposed to the spiritual or intellectual. You live in a world surrounded by having and holding possessions. It is claimed that you become distracted from intellectual pursuits by material things, and yet you continual to invent, innovate and produce measurable goods.

This is a cycle of creativity, production, and usage that would be lost if we tried to live a minimalistic life.

There is an old saying that money can't buy happiness, but money gives you the opportunity to provide your family with experiences. Commercialism or holding possessions is not as terrible as the minimalists claim. Commercialism has definite redeeming values since the world's economy is based on physical goods.

Materialism

Materialism is holding possessions for physical comfort, but having stuff is meaningful. Like it or not, finding meaning in stuff is important, and finding stuff you love is important. Citizens find creation through possessions. Mankind has always been on a quest to find and create meaningful objects. Possessing and creating is what inspires human achievements. The human mindset always quests for stuff - magic rings, beautiful artwork, the Golden Fleece, and so much more. Without materialism, there would be no creativity.

We thrive in a materialist society. Children learn and flourish when they live in a steady home with their possessions around them. Their possessions give them psychological security. Having things around provides a comfort zone. You can rest and recharge your batteries and energies when you own physical items that are significant to you.

Of course, materialism, as well as commercialism, has problems. Obsession with stuff tends to make consumers hoarders. It forces you to seek continually for something better, more fulfilling, and emotionally satisfying. You look for instant gratification in purchasing and holding stuff. Perhaps the clue to keeping materialism from taking over your life is to determine when enough is enough. That is not minimalism, however, but practicality.

We live in a world surrounded by composed stuff. C.S. Lewis once said, "God ... likes matter. He invented it." It is natural to become distracted from spiritual pursuits by seeking to have possessions, but it is equally as spiritual to use your material possessions to obtain happiness for yourself and for others (AllAboutPhilosophy, 2015).

There is nothing wrong with having and holding possessions. The Bible is full of stories of those who own much. How do minimalists reconcile God's riches with a desire to live a minimalist lifestyle? "God's home, the Temple, was adorned with gold beyond imagination" (Ps50:10).

Minimalism vs Materialism

Becoming a minimalist and living an intentional lifestyle can be difficult. Before committing your stuff to the garbage, you need to determine why this counter-cultural is for you. Think through the impact that minimalism will have on your family and their lifestyle before you begin on a journey of randomly de-cluttering.

As an example, one young husband decided that his small family would become minimalists. His wife disagreed with him. She had no problem with decluttering or organizing, but she put her foot down on doing away with family valuables, hobbies, and expensive children's toys. The young husband insisted that minimalism would save their lives. The family could not come to a consensus of how to de-clutter, what to discard, and which lifestyle was best. The family split and went their minimalist and materialistic ways.

There are those who have become minimalists because of constant blogs, newsletters, suggestions, and arguments. One author finally determined that the trend to be a minimalist was the right path for her.

The author decided to declutter her life. She gritted her teeth and cleaned out her possesses to the point where her house was very sparse and very minimal. After finishing this task of de-cluttering, she looked around and realized that minimalism was not who she was. She wanted to be surrounded by things; stuff that moved her to create. Tabletops piled with books and candles, mantles filled with pictures and treasures, and a china closet with all the wonderful keepsakes from her childhood. These were the things that defined who she was. She frantically began searching for her lost goods and let possessions back into her life. Her home is no longer clutter free but filled with wonderful stuff that defines who she is (Roth, 2011).

Minimalism is more than just throwing away possessions and doing away with clutter. It is a journey that could just turn you into a miserable miser.   You must first decide within yourself why you have been keeping stuff. Discovering the reasons for minimalism is an emotional process. It could be very painful. As in the previous example, stuff defines you.

Minimalism is bringing to the forefront the things you most value and getting rid of those things that are nonessential. Prioritize your essential values and write them down. You will probably come to the conclusion you are much happier with possessions than without them.

The world was intended to produce, promote and invent material possessions. These inventions were intended for the good of society. By giving away all your possessions and refusing to acquire things, you are acting totally selfish. You deny invention, production, and employment to others who need to create, invent, and produce.

Once you have set on the path of minimalism, you will rock friendships and relationships. Minimalism will become a topic of conversation and people will initially be intrigued by your new lifestyle. They will ask you how you got to this point of giving away possessions. You will definitely enjoy speaking about the positive impact this decision has made on your life, and you will try to inflict this lifestyle on others. People will not be impressed; they will be irritated. Think about becoming a minimalist. If you find that really want this lifestyle, then by all means become a minimalist. If you want to be a citizen who follows trends, avoid trying to convince those who love their possessions to take on your new lifestyle.

Materialism and owning possessions are not a complete source of happiness, but they aren't a cause of unhappiness. When the man on his deathbed says, "I wish I spent more time with my family instead of working so hard," is not claiming that material possessions are unimportant. He is expressing that his obsessions with material things was wrong. Money and material stuff are quite neutral. Stuff is a very powerful tool in achieving happiness if you take care not to let accumulating wealth hurt those you love. Take another example of a family with a cabin. Every year they take a long vacation to their cabin. They form great memories and are happy. They get to know each other and learn to play together. The cabin does not make them happy, but the experiences shared at the cabin do. Their trick was not letting work get in the way. It took extra sacrifices to build their cabin, but family relationships were not one of their sacrifices. They worked together.   Most people love their possessions – their families, homes, cars, and careers. Where would we be without our summer bbq on the patio or going out to eat or to the movies? Personally, having things makes most people happy.

The statement, "Money can't buy happiness, but it can buy marshmallows which are sort of the same thing," is tongue-in-cheek, but it is real. Money can buy stuff that makes one happy.

Minimalism can drive you Crazy

Let's be honest; minimalism can drive you crazy. Following the full philosophy of minimalism means you have no compulsion to plan for your future. You give away all your belongings, save nothing for retirement and end up living in a cheap apartment and in a very poor area of town. Your books, music, and art are things of the past. Being a minimalist will not give you the joy in taking a road trip or planning for a happy life. You have no car, little money, and no way to travel.

There would be nothing to help you feel secure. You would essentially live a bohemian lifestyle with very little on the walls of your home to prove that you really existed.

Minimalism makes you complacent. You own less therefore you do less. You look to find happiness with very little and this in turn forces you to strive less to upgrade your life. Finding happiness in having little sounds intriguing, but what you are doing is checking out of the race of life, and stifling ambition. You no longer want to win the race; you just move as simply as you can through the years.

Minimalism is squandering your opportunities. You have the ability to have anything you want, but you throw it away in the name of minimalism. Life is meaningless unless you have little. Those who are minimalist due to circumstances think you are crazy for actively shunning all of your opportunities. Those with little would gladly give you their poor and meaningless life to have the opportunities to own something significant.

Minimalism encourages short-term thinking, a loss of investing, and an eventual destruction of the economy. Minimalists claim that possessions should not define who you are. But that is exactly what possessions do; they define you. Are you known as the guy with the awesome car? That is a possession and a definition. Are you an artist with a studio full of incredible art? Or are you are the corporate ladder climber; that is your definition, and who you are. Living a minimalist lifestyle would demand that you get rid of your car and your art or even give up your high-powered job. Go ahead and give up these opportunities and things. You are now without your identity.

Balance Minimalism with Materialism/Commercialism

A true minimalist counts their possessions. They are honest about what they own. They believe you only need a few things you frequently use. This lack of possessions, say minimalists, will ultimately give you an appreciation of what you do have.

Not really. In fact, trying to get rid of possessions will ultimately throw you into a competition with other minimalists. You try to get rid of more than they do.

It becomes a cycle of who has less.

Try literally counting everything you own. Counting includes the clocks in your home, your toothbrush, photos, the trash under the sink and the salt and pepper shakers. Count your cooking utensils and the rack that holds your cleaning supplies Count your furniture. Group your underwear, clothing, hangers, and food. Count your books. Just keep going and you will fill up pages and pages of things you own. Now take this huge list and start paring it down. Throw out duplicate items, the things you found that you no longer use. Determine what you will need and what you will give or throw away. Throwing out stuff and trying to determine what is valuable is a great exercise. It is also highly time-consuming, and depressing.

You can be a "minimalist" without throwing everything away. Live within your means and learn to live with possessions that can shield you from economic shocks and instability. Appreciate what you do have and strive to make your life better by consolidating and decluttering. There are always possessions you don't need and can get rid of to make your life richer. Determining what is needed and what is not, is not minimalist living; it is being practical.   As minimalism grows in popularity, more and more people are turning to minimalism. They have bought into the philosophy that focusing less on possessions and more on experiences will bring happiness. It also is a philosophy that leads to the mediocre. "What is the least I can do and still get by?" Use that statement as a tool in the core parts of your lives. You have now succeeded in becoming boring, unfulfilled, and unexceptional. Minimalism is a mindset and can quickly become a habit the swings out of control. It is a principle that is never ending. You are always trying to do the least you can do to get by. "What is the least I can do and still get to heaven?" "What is the least I can do to keep my job?" (Fallible, 2014).)

Minimalism breeds a lack of passion. It is a character disease and the enemy of excellence. "Minimalism is a cancer on society," Matthew Kelly, The Rhythm of Life.

Procrastination is minimalism at its worst. For example if you are not disciplined and trying to get things done, you make up for it by doing the very least you can do. You cut corners and get though using easy and minimalist ways. Being a minimalist and doing only the basics or wanting only the basics brings on the mindset of wanting the fruits of a job or position, but avoiding the work.   Minimalism can be bad for your health. Take for example the minimalist who has very little furniture, but what he does have is polished to such a high gleam that it resembles a show home. The kitchen is so spotless you could operate in it. Such cleanliness and minimalism discourage normal human activity. If you cannot act like a normal human being in your own home, then abnormal behavior takes over. Mildly obsessive or even compulsive obsessive behavior will not allow you to enjoy the fruits of your labors. Minimalist decorating believes that your furniture must remain shop-worthy, and floors touched by only clean bare feet. Don't let this happen to your home, scuffs and stains are signs of a life embraced and enjoyed. Trying to be minimalist so you do not have to continually clean and pick up causes anxiety (Carver, 2011).

Cons of Minimalism

How you approach your lifestyle will determine the best way for you to live. There are awesome aspects to minimalism, but there are just as many downsides. Get rid of your television and you have freed up several hours a day. Now you have more time to spend on iPad games, doing nothing productive, or wandering the streets looking for other simple people.

You will have few houseguests. Your home is too quiet with no radio or television, you have nowhere for them to sleep, and you have little food in the house.

Get rid of stuff and declutter. However, the downside is becoming obsessed with counting your stuff and trying to subtract it from your life. You become almost manic in your lack of possessions. You search for more things to get rid of and finally end up getting rid of your happy life.

Who wants to live in a boring house? When you reduce your stuff to the bare essentials, you have nothing to make you happy, pleased, or passionate.

As you live with less, you gain more confidence in experiences and living with less. The downside to this philosophy is the arrogance you develop. You live with less and look down on others who work very hard to have possessions.   Slow down, get rid of the cell phone, find a way to limit activities, and become less stressed. Easy to say, but how do you tell your children that they can no longer play soccer, baseball or take swimming lessons. What will you replace these activities with? Mindlessly trying to remove more possessions from your home?

People will think you are about to commit suicide. This is a shocking reason, but when you quickly get rid of stuff, people think the worst.

You will be blamed for the unemployment rate rising

because have less stuff, you buy less stuff, and therefore you cause people to lose their jobs. This is the Law of Unintended Consequences. (This law is the unintended consequences caused by the action of people. It is maintained that each individual seeking only his own gain or lack of "gain is led by an invisible hand to promote an end that was no part of his intention" (Norton, 2014).

Everyone you know will tell you to hold on to things "just in case." They you're your to spot throwing away stuff. You feel just the opposite. You want to get rid of stuff and their ideas cause you anxiety.

If everyone cut their consumption, the economy would all apart. The jobless rate would rise. More people would be unable to buy food or pay their rents and mortgages. The economy should serve us, but we make the economy what it is. Without commercialism, there would be no economy.

If everyone created and no one consumed, creativity would quickly come to a standstill. Minimalism as well as materialism hinges on the law of supply and demand. Demand for stuff is high right now so more stuff must be created and produced, creating more jobs.

Minimalism states that stuff needs to be thrown out. Where does it go? Most goes to landfills, some is reused and other stuff is recycled. Consumers, and this includes minimalists, are lazy. They toss garbage into the trash bin rather than consciously recycling. The trash goes to the landfill and causes environmental damages.   Running children to ball games, swimming lessons and play dates are family's entertainment. What is more awesome than cheering for your Little League Team or being a part of a swim meet? Would you deny your children these experiences so you can live a minimalist life? Your pace of life has slowed down considerably since you have cut the excess from your life. It is less stressful for you, but everyone else in your family is miserable. You really need to get real and understand that life is not about being simple. Life is complicated, full of activity, and fulfilling.

Duplicity exists in everyone's world. You have one life that is surrounded by friends and family, another life that is dependent on your co-workers, and another life that is your solitary life. You play a different role depending on your where you are at the moment. Minimalism stresses taking all these parts of your life out of the picture. You lose the variety that makes you, you.

People always become someone different as circumstances change. You need to learn how to be compatible. Being a minimalist prevents situational changes. As a minimalist, you are required to be the same no matter where you are. You have no opportunity to be different, learn and grow. Minimalism demands you get rid of duplicity, but now you are a one-dimensional person. Minimalism does call out for one to be simpler and quieter, and that is good. Do slow down, consume less, but enjoy more. Continue, however, chasing the dream ring that is just out of reach. Striving, chasing, and searching for dreams gives you personality and excitement. Most people realize that life is not movies, books, or celebrity magazines. It is simple and touchable. Becoming a minimalist, however, means you let go of your questing for something better and become flat and boring.

Minimalism is completely achievable. If you desire few possessions in your life, then discard them. Just remember that unless you totally rid your world of possessions, thoughts and emotions you will never be a true minimalist. You will just be confused.

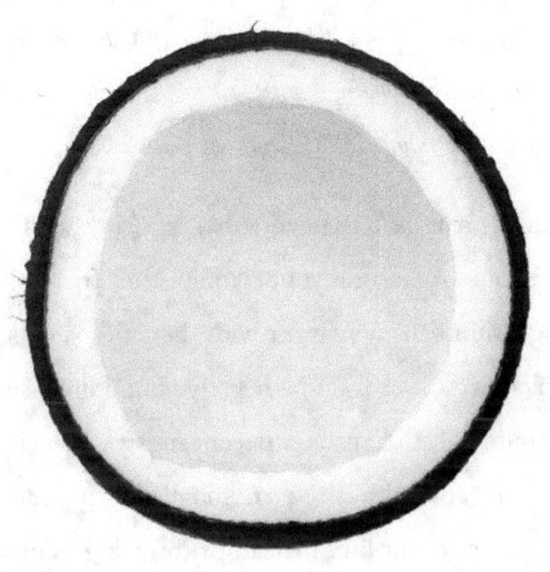

Chapter III: Minimalism is Not For Everyone

"It's quite simple: to be a minimalist you must live with less than 100 things, you can't own a car or a home or a television, you can't have a career, you must live in exotic hard-to-pronounce places all over the world, you must start a blog, you can't have children, and you must be a young white male from a privileged background." ~Millburn & Nicodemus

Minimalism is not for everyone. It is not a lifestyle you should pressure your family and friends into trying. Minimalism may provide benefits, and some people have never found a negative in minimalism. In fact, minimalism can be a decent lifestyle, but if you are not committed to minimalism it can be devastating to our life. Instead of throwing things out willy-nilly, take stock of what possessions are important to you.

Minimalism has many parameters. Going from owning 10,000 things to only owning 7,000 can be minimalism. Cleaning out your closet to contain only one t-shirt may be minimalism to you. Your lifestyle is a totally personal choice. If you have a particular personality trait, however, you should never consider minimalism. For example:

Collectors. If you own a collection of items and these possession bring you joy, this collection is part of your personality. No one should talk you into throwing away you collections. You will be miserable and come to resent your newfound way of life. For example, a good friend down the road has a collection of over 1000 salt and pepper shakers. If she were to throw them away, a part of her life would be thrown away with her collection. Perhaps she should stop purchasing more salt and pepper shakers, but this stuff are her memories from her world travels.

Fashionistas. Fashion is a part of a personality. If it fits and you love it; keep it. It is your choice what passions to keep. When your job or career depends on how you dress, keep all the fashions that match your job. You never know when you will need a piece of clothing for a project. Organize your closet to keep you fashions easy to find.

If you are a **photographer**, you should never throw away equipment. It does not matter if you have a plethora of cameras and lighting equipment; they are important to your well-being. Keep them, organize them, and love them. The same with photographs, you should not let the minimalism lifestyle dictate what pictures you throw away and which ones you keep.

Mechanics need stuff. What would happen if you threw away your tools to make room for experiences? You would shortly be out of a job and a great deal of money.

If you are on a relationship break, it might not be a good idea to throw out every item that reminds you of your ex-significant other. You never know when or if you get back together. If would be so devastating to the other partner if they discovered you had thrown away that Oriental vase they so lovingly bought for you.

Children should not be forced into a minimalist lifestyle. The possessions they hold are their security nets. Children's rooms are their havens and to them minimalism is just a word. Children will eventually de-clutter their lives.

Let them make the choice between minimalism and materialism when they understand the terms, and when they are much older.

Your loved ones may support you in your minimalist lifestyle, but they have their own preferences and experiences. They are on a different path and materialism may be their preference. Sharing an opinion and offering an option about de-cluttering, organizing and simplifying is great, but demanding that your loved ones join you on the minimalism journey is not good. Conflicts between family members and heated arguments can happen. Don't force your minimalist ideas on your roommates. If your roommate wants to purchase hundreds of shoes, music or cooking utensils, that is awesome. Preferences are what makes a person.

If you are a family man or woman, minimalism is not a good idea. Giving up all your possessions will take away a place to call home. The things you are quite attached to will be gone, or you will have to rent a storage unit.

A highly competitive person can be dangerous with minimalism. Mankind has a deeply-rooted drive to compete with each other and advertising capitalizes on this impulse.

What do you take pride in? Purchasing the newest thing gives you the right to belong to the club of consumers. You are measured on what you have. For a moment your life's problems are gone because you have stuff. Now turn to minimalism. You are that person who looks down on everyone who owns things. You compete with your neighbors to see who can get rid of stuff the fastest. You don't think about what you are doing; only the end result. After the "game" is over you sit and look around you. There is nothing more to get rid of and your life is empty. Now you start the competition again. You begin to purchase what you threw out. A vicious cycle begins all over (Smith, 2013).

If you want to give your children an awesome future and if you are a minimalist, it will be difficult to save for your children's education or even help them when they need a place to stay. Making sure they learn without being bullied for their lifestyle or clothes requires a nesting place and stuff.

 Life is a balance and taking minimalism too far disturbs that balance. "Flowing too much in the direction of simplicity could lead you to feeling deprived" (minimalismissimple, 2015).

A good point to make, "When you call yourself a minimalist, everything you do will be instantly be steeped in irony" (Millburn & Nicodemus, 2015). Do you really want to have people think of you as a hypocrite? They will if you have more than one pair of shoes or drive a car or own a blowdryer.

Find a balance in living that becomes you. You don't need to reject every item that is given to you to keep your life simple. Instead, carefully choose what you will allow into your life. Thinking about what to purchase and what ideals to follow is a good motto to follow in every aspect of your life. If you deprive yourself, you may find that you are unsatisfied and unhappy. Unhappiness could lead to splurges and a vicious cycle of minimalism versus materialism begins.

Keep your possessions. Materialism and having possessions is a decision. It is a choice to live in today's culture. Advertising, marketing campaigns, and corporations exist for you to consume, collect and purchase. Every message heard in advertisements promotes being happy if you have the latest and greatest in appliances, cars, homes, furnishing, and fashions. The world's economy runs on materialism. Suddenly discovering you need to get rid of possessions may enact a terrible price from you. You have always known where your recycling bin or garbage can is, but you still have your possessions. Decluttering is good for the soul, but only if it is your decision. Being forced to get rid of possessions hurts, and who wants to hurt?

Minimalism is the intentional promotion of the things you value and removing anything that is a distraction from your life. You will need to identify the essentials and prioritize those essentials. Minimalism will demand that you come to the realization that you have spent much of your life pursuing things that are not that valuable. Materialism will help you justify keeping those possessions.

Do you really want to rock your view of society, you lifestyle, your relationships or areas of your life that you never thought possible? Or do you enjoy what you have? The world invents, produces, promotes and purchases material possessions to keep the economy running. We love stuff. Stuff is security, needed to impress neighbors and prove your worth. If you want to change your view of possessions, become a minimalist, but if you are happy with your view of society, culture, and its messages stay where you are.   People who have become minimalists have said that they wish they had never taken the step. Testimonials from Melissa, Di and Christine say "I live without means and I don't get to live life as freely as others. My family and friends are non-supportive. There are times when I thought I'd never survive. Being a minimalist complicates my life. I need my things back."

Try and have an open mind when someone is talking to you about minimalism. They might love their perspective, but not everyone is interested in living the same lifestyle, and that's what makes life interesting. If a minimalist constantly tells you what is wrong with your possession filled life, just let them talk. Do support them in their lifestyle, but remember that you are happy owning stuff.

Practical minimalism might be your means to a comfortable and fulfilling existence. Downsize your stuff if it will make sense for you and your lifestyle. Avoid throwing away and decluttering without thinking through the issues, and never get rid of your stuff when you are angry. If you would like to live a simple lifestyle that is awesome, but take the "religious fervor" out of the movement and make the transition at your own pace.

Chapter IV: Minimalism versus Frugal Living

"Extreme minimalism is akin to extreme frugality: It works for some people, but robs others of life's dear enjoyments." ~ J.D. Roth

Being frugal is not the same as being a minimalist. Frugality is being careful with your money. Minimalism is decluttering and getting rid of stuff. The two concepts do intersect, you save money and de-clutter at the same time, but they are not the same thing.   Minimalism is not living like a monk; it is simple living with less. You have thrown away the stuff in our home and in your mind to make room for values and experiences. Minimalism is not about being thrifty; it is a tool to help you change your lifestyle. The entire idea of minimalism and frugality joined together is to live a more intentional life. Focus less on the material things of life, save money, and do not own more than you need and can use (The Everyday Minimalist, 2010).

There are similarities and differences between frugality and minimalism. Decluttering and minimizing possessions are philosophies used in both lifestyles, but how does a minimalist justify the frugal practice of purchasing in bulk and storing for a rainy day?

Frugality is thriftiness and moderate or even slightly pious living. A frugal person will cut corners to save money, make adjustments, and understand the cost-per-use and the longevity of purchase. They do have possessions and value what they have. Possessions contribute to their frugality and may be sparce and minimal.

Minimalism is about embracing and maximizing the important things of life and distancing yourself from the less important things around you. "Minimalism is a tool used to rid yourself of life's excess in favor of focusing on what is important so you can find happiness, fulfillment and freedom (Millburn & Nicodemus, 2015).

Minimalism is designed to add value to lives by clearing the clutter out of your life to make room for health, relationships, passion, contribution, and growth.

A minimalist would not purchase an expensive pair of shoes just because they are well made and last longer, as would a frugal shopper. A minimalist would not even purchase an additional pair of shoes.

Frugality

Frugality is living a lifestyle where luxury is rare and hedonism, or pleasure-seeking, is completely unheard of and discouraged. Socks are darned rather than replaced, holes in jeans are patched up and hand me downs were in everyone's closet. Meals are basic and everything is saved. Definitely a truly frugal lifestyle can be closed and uncomfortable, but it is not minimalist.   Being frugal is all about saving money and spending less than you make. Frugal living means being prudent or economical in the consumption of resources and avoiding waste, lavishness and extravagance. Reduce waste, curb costly habits and suppress instant gratification by means of self-restraint. Frugal living seeks to find efficiency and stays well informed about local circumstances. A frugal life is one that avoid products that are "for the moment". The premise is to gain the most from money.   Learning to live on a modest income, shop at yard sales and thrift stores, and being adept at stretching out dollars are the keys to frugal living. Living frugal does not mean getting rid of possessions. In fact, every possession is important. Thrift is important, and low cost entertainment is a way of life.

Frugal people are not necessarily minimalists. Many thrifty people have no desire to be minimalists. They believe that holding onto things "just in case" is being frugal. Holding on to stuff in order to avoid purchasing the same item is smart. Shopping bargains is a way of life with a frugal lifestyle, and shopping thrift stores and estates sales is a hobby.

Choosing Your Lifestyle

Minimalism is getting rid of excess, decluttering, and living a simple life. The philosophy of minimalism stresses having less to deal with in the way of possessions and living a less complicated life. Minimalism and frugal living are similar in the viewpoint that buying less reduces the amount of items that are overproduced. Thinking about excess stuff causes you to repurpose and re-use what you already own.

Minimalism is similar to frugality by emphasizing savings through having less. Buying less frequently means spending less and having fewer possessions to take maintain. As you pick and choose what is important to you, you also have less wasted time. You can live simpler in a modern world by utilizing frugalism and minimalism. It is also possible to live a happy and simple life by being a consumer and finding ways to increase those things that make you happy. If you want to live a simple life and sit on a lake enjoying nature, that is an awesome dream. So is sailing on a lake in a sailboat or running through waves on a water ski. A neighbor recently said, "I live a minimalist life in my cabin by the lake. Only the bare essentials are there and I am supremely happy. I can also choose to stay at home in my suburban home that is full of all the amenities that I love, the television, my hot tub, and my hobbies." How awesome to change lifestyle whenever you need a change of pace.

There are things you can do to simplify your life, be frugal and minimalistic, and still enjoy possessions.

Get a basic cell phone. Just use it for emergencies. However if you need one to take pictures, text, and search for places to go, you smartphone is your frugal investment.

Cut the cable cord. You can save a ton of money without cable or satellite. Instead use free sites and add a steaming service. Not only is his frugal and minimalist, it is smart – you can control what your children watch.

Get rid of credit cards if you are seeking a simpler

life. However, if you have an emergency it is a good idea to have a credit card on standby. That is smart and frugal living.

Declutter your home.
Okay, you don't need three brooms and having a multitude of the same tools is a bit overdone. You could get rid of duplicates and find space on shelves and in drawers.

If you don't use your gym membership, mobile internet service, or milk delivery service, it is smart to get rid of them. This is the hallmark of a frugal life – getting rid of excess to save money.   Track your expenses and time. See where you are wasting money and time. This is a concept that can make life simpler and still give you the opportunity to be a consumer. Living a smarter life is not necessarily becoming a minimalist or adopting a frugal lifestyle, it is keeping the things you love, purchasing the things you need, and living a sensible life.

Chapter V: Minimalism and Your Diet

"Minimalism means not trying to improve perfection." That includes diet. ~Bryant McGill

It might seem strange to combine minimalism and diet, but if you are getting rid of physical clutter, you might as well go all the way and take food out of your life that is unhealthy for you. Being a true minimalist does mean turning toward a diet of little meat or becoming a vegetarian.

A minimalist does not complicate their diet any more than they complicate their life. They do have a few essential rules the follow to stay minimally and healthy.

Food that consists mostly of plants and unprocessed food is definitely good for anyone – minimalist or materialist. Eat an abundance of vegetables like avocados, spinach, broccoli, and anything else that is green. These foods will make you feel wonderful. Put fish, nuts and seeds into your minimalist/everyday diet. Keep the portions on the small side, or minimal.

Completely eliminate from your diet, breads, pastas, sugar, gluten and meat that is not fish, avoid bottom feeding seafood like shrimp and crab, and stay away from most dairy products. Do not purchase or eat anything that is processed or packaged. If you are contemplating a minimalist lifestyle think about giving up those candy bars and sugary sodas. A minimalist believes that you need less protein than you think.

Fasting is great if you are a minimalist. Dogmatic minimalists eat only two meals a day and stay away from snacks. During the fast a minimalist diet is water, herbal, tea or black coffee. You definitely will lose weight. A minimalist diet does not include breakfast.

This is contrary to dietary recommendations. Breakfast is the fuel of the day. Whether you are a minimalist or not, never skip breakfast.

Keep your sugars to a minimum and your water and liquids to a maximum. With a minimalist diet you do need to take supplements. Multivitamins, vitamin B-complex and fish oil will need to be purchased so make sure you have the resources on hand to buy these ingredients for your minimalist diet.   Exercise is on the schedule of a minimalist. Minimalists don't spend a great deal of time, effort or focus on exercising. They walk since waking allows plenty of time to think and de-stress. They sometimes work out for fifteen minutes. Minimalists are not concerned about building vanity muscles, they are only concerned with how they feel in the moment.

If you have a gym pass, keep it simple and use it. You don't have to follow the minimalist ideal of exercise; do what you think is best for your own lifestyle and body.

Sleep is important to a minimalists, just like it is important for anyone. A minimalist tends to sleep less because they only need five or six hours of sleep. Do get as much sleep as your body requires and turn of the alarm clock. You don't have a stressful job anyway, so why hurry and get up.

Less stress is the result of a minimalist diet, sleep, exercise, and lifestyle. You can tell a minimalist because they do not shallow breathe, never frown, and make an effort to be aware of the triggers that bring on stress. Minimalists learn to change their breathing patterns when they feel overwhelmed. One trick to being less stressed? Look in the mirror and smile at yourself

Steps to a Minimalist Diet, Even if you are not a Minimalist

Apply minimalism to your diet by Minimizing portions.

Eat small portions. Eat half your meal when at restaurants and use smaller plats at home. Avoid second helpings. This is a great way to control your food, but somewhat wasteful.

Eat half your meal when at restaurants and throw away the rest? Maybe just order less. What about second portions at thanksgiving or family dinners? Do you really want to insult your relatives by not taking a second helping? And really, what does not taking a second helping have to do with minimalist living?

Minimize eating unhealthy food. This is actually good advice. Reduce the extra sour cream and bacon on baked potatoes and eat the skin. Add more fruits and vegetables to your diet.

Avoid snacking. Choose very small portions when snacking. If you have a minimalist near you when you are snacking take after them and eat only one nut. This idea is somewhat sarcastic, but when you are minimalist snacking, it is a great idea to follow the "less is more" mantra.

Water should be everyone beverage of choice. Drink more water and cut down on the sodas, sugary fruit juices, and caffeinated drinks. This is great advice for anyone living a material or a minimalist life. Empty calories have no nutrition. Avoid them. Applying minimalism to foods and drinks means eliminating toxins and junk including artificially flavored or colored beverage (West, 2015).

Eat when hungry. Schedules are obsessive and make your life complicated. Simplify your life and eat only when you are hungry. "If the tank is still left with fuel, minimalists are simply not obsessed with filling it up. They know Eco is the trend, they wait till it's nearly empty, then get it refilled" (Xuan, 2011). Stop when you are full. Whenever they eat, a minimalist won't stuff themselves. Their motto is enough is enough.

There are tasty foods everywhere you look. You can never eat them all and a minimalist will not want to get involved in craving foods. They pass up great looking food to keep themselves simple. Nice idea, but if you love food, it is okay to indulge once in a while.

When a minimalist eats, they eat with full attention to detail. They savor the flavors and textures and eat slowly and joyfully. They experience their food rather just fill themselves up. Nothing is eaten in a hurry. What a great premise! Eat for enjoyment rather than gorging yourself.

A full and tight stomach is something that a minimalist will not tolerate. Minimalists keep themselves light in food, as well as their furnishings, thoughts and emotions.

Minimalists claim that by simplifying their lives they have more time to get into shape. No matter what lifestyle you are living, getting into shape is a need rather than a want; it is not "a should, but a must." Use minimalistic principles to get rid of life's excess so you can focus on what's important. Take this same motto to heart.

Chapter VI: How to Become A Hybrid Minimalist

"Owning less is better than organizing more." ~ Joshua Becker

There is a very definite cycle in the modern world. You work hard, make tons of money, and purchase all the things you have dreamed. Now you work harder to keep all your possessions in good order. You are trapped in a job you don't really like, but you need to pay for the lifestyle you have become accustomed. You are determined to make your life work which causes stress, ulcers, back problems, and unhappiness.

Another scenario, you work hard during the week at a job you enjoy. The weekend or days off come, and you are able to use the stuff you have worked hard to purchase. You love your life of owning a boat, a nice house and an awesome car. You know possessions are fleeting, but they give you pleasure and contentment.

Everyone has a different way to be happy. We value different things and what we own aligns to our own personal ethics. Materialism or minimalism, it doesn't matter. Look at your life and see whether the way your life is in position with your values, your wants and desires, and your happiness. If you find that stuff is crowding your life; pare it down. If your inner peace asks you to rejoice over your next big deal, then have a party and celebrate your "stuff". Your inner peace, or the state of being you create within yourself, is what is important. It should not matter what philosophy is trending or whether or not people think you are materialistic (Logue, 2015).

Extreme or dogmatic minimalism involves living with very few possessions; often less than 100 items. Forming your minimalist life makes you happy. You long to follow the premise of getting rid of material possessions and uncomplicated your life. You believe that your stuff drains your bank accounts, your energy, and attention. Possessions keep you from enjoying the ones you love and living a life based purely on values. This type of minimalism would be difficult for anyone to follow unless you are unattached and jobless.

At the same time you are trying to keep your stuff under control which causes you to become a slave to minimums. Your life and lifestyle becomes unfulfilling and stressful. Are you any happier than the individual who works hard and purchases stuff? The answer lies in moderation. Many minimalists turn to rational or balanced minimalism to reconcile their needs and wants. Rather than the term minimalist that conjures up images of barren walls, destitution, and empty cupboards, a rational minimalist balances what they have. They organize, de-clutter, and put together a plan for simplicity. A minimalist family who lives a minimalist lifestyle, owns a television, couches, family photos, and chairs. This family has more than one coat to wear and t-shirts overflow drawers. There are books, crafts, and toys in different rooms of their home. What they do have is an organized home and items that are not duplicates. They define what a minimalist lifestyle means to them — having only the essentials and determining themselves what those essentials are. They have established a life that is not identical to anybody else's; it is their life and theirs alone, and they call it minimalism   Becoming a minimalist or following a materialistic lifestyle requires that you develop the style to fit your needs. Ask questions, and identify what you most value. Be humble enough to change when necessary. Every practice of minimalism must look different from anyone else's. If you are a collector of antiques, stamps or salt and pepper shakers and you love music and movies plus sports and books, you can keep them in your minimalist lifestyle. Minimalist living should be based on your values, passions, and desires. Be rational.

The world of work feeds your desires for ambition and wanting more. How do you balance your ambitions, have a successful career, without losing your contentment and getting drawn into a cycle of purchasing, maintaining, and hoarding? One answer would be finding a job you like, one are good at doing, a job that pays well, and a job that brings out satisfaction, and friendships.

Finding balance in minimalism takes teamwork. Don't be dismayed if you make many mistakes along the way. Balance what you have with what you need and remove those unneeded things from your life. Find space to promote the things you most value; remove distractions. Learn to balance your life between the extremes of consumerism and extreme minimalism.

Balance minimalism with having stuff and keep your attitude to yourself. Yes, minimalism has become the new rage, and it is trendy to say, we don't have a TV." How often have your heard this statement said with a haughty attitude. Yet, you see these same minimalists allowing children to play in the street.

Forced minimalism is when you are coerced into minimizing because of a job loss, divorce, legal action or homelessness. You give everything away to the point that all you have, maybe, is a bed and one blanket. Forced minimalism will not make you happy; it is not a good situation.

Not everyone who embraces minimalism takes the philosophy to the limit. You don't really have to sacrifice your precious stuff. All you need to do is take advantage of all getting rid of excess and having an attitude of living with only what you need.

Minimalism advocates experiences. No one disputes the idea that experiences are long lasting, but what if the things you purchase are what makes the memories? Everything you own and value should represent something: memories, happy times, family get reunions and learning, achieving and receiving. This lifestyle might work well for a single person who travels quite a bit and has no permanent home, but it is much more difficult for a family to practice extreme minimalism.

Balance your life by getting rid of items that are of little or no use and keep items that are useful in a day to day life. Cleaning out stuff is the beginning of living a balanced but minimal life.   Equalize your life by being practical. Being a practical minimalist means you still have stuff, but you think about what you have. You make tangible choices and think about what you are doing. The result can be a weight lifted from your life. Declutter mindfully and slowly. Don't let the change overwhelm you or your family.

A Balanced Materialist Lifestyle

Live your materialistic life. Your possessions may define who you are, and that's okay. Have an awareness of what is around you and notice how things really are. Just avoid worshipping materials things, possessions, and money. Let your stuff work for you instead of against you. You can use your material possessions to experience life and do the things you love and value.

Society urges us to be consumers. You become a working class citizen to make enough money to enjoy possessions. To balance this concept, you don't need to become a minimalist, you just need to be smart. Purchase what you need and want and take care of it. Avoid worshipping stuff. Stuff is just stuff, and it can be replaced.

Buying stuff is not a bad thing. Purchasing runs the economy. If you enjoy spending $150 on a pair of leather shoes that will last you at least years, then this is your happiness. If you need to have a smart phone, video games or a television to be happy, that is your bliss. The whole idea to living a minimalist lifestyle is to find a way to stop giving so much meaning to your stuff. Again, let your stuff work for you, not the other way around.

Balance materialism with the things you want. Make all the money you can. Money is important, and use that money not only for materialistic things, but to maintain a balance with spirituality and giving. Money is important for happiness. It may not be the most essential component of happiness, but could you really say that a homeless beggar is truly happy even though he is living a minimalist lifestyle?   Everyone wants to succeed, do better, and improve their lives. Minimalists would be liars if they denied wanted to improve. Their whole life depends on improvement and change.

Every year that technology increases you purchase bigger and better things for you and your family. You experience them, use them for good, and are proud of what you have purchased. Would you really like to turn the clock back one hundred years and live a minimalist lifestyle without the conveniences of a modern, materialistic life?   Materialism is also an attitude. Learning to balance minimalism with materialism means you get rid of things that you don't use anymore, and you pass your stuff to others who can use them. Repurpose, recycle, and reuse. The joy of minimalism is hanging on to your precious stuff and memories, but letting go of past items that bring your distress.

 Refocusing your life off of materials possession and workaholic actions, to your family. Avoid maintaining all your stuff; get rid of things that re not useful. Minimalism states, when the unnecessary stuff is gone, you have less maintenance, and you can focus your time and energy on those possessions and people that are important to you.

Balance materialism and having stuff by getting rid of the stuff you don't use and trade it in for items you will use. For example, if you have a boat sitting in the driveway that is costing you in registration and maintenance fees and you never use this boat, sell it. Purchase something that will bring joy and experiences to your family.   Simplify your workload.

Think about every project and obligation you are asked to do. Don't pile work on top of work. Make a choice in the projects you take on before agree to more obligations. Drop those useless things that do not mean much in your life. Letting go of extra activities can give you more time to pursue your passions, and get the most of your life.

Get rid of toxic and boring relationships from your life. Surround yourself with people who think like you and have substance. Get rid of those people in your social media lists who do nothing for you. Spend time with the people you love who enrich your life. Balance your stuff with your emotions, friends, and relationships. Find equilibrium between living as a minimalist or a materialistic life. Do this by determining what is important to you.

Learn to love what you do for work and money. There are many people who have high paying jobs that they love. They don't squander their money on stuff that is meaningless. They save for the things they want and are happy saving and planning. There are many more people who know how to organize, live simply, yet hold stuff.

Balance in Decluttering and Organizing

The problem with decluttering and turning to a minimalist lifestyle is the stuff just doesn't disappear. The results of your de-cluttering and cleaning up needs to go somewhere. There is no way to decrease or increase the matter in the universe. Stuff just rearranges and moves to someplace else. You are not a minimalist when you just toss our stuff into the trash. You have now selfishly rid yourself of possessions, and placed this stuff somewhere else. Perhaps the answer to becoming a minimalist is to seek to move things that are out of place to where they might best be used (Rich, 2011).

In the book Simplify by Joshua Becker (a minimalist blogger), there are seven guiding principles to help anyone declutter their home and mind. While it is true that getting rid of clutter is awesome, what do you do if you have gotten rid of items that you occasionally need? Recently a new minimalist was looking for a great cut class bowl to take to a party. Of course, since it was not used or needed, it had been discarded. It was at the moment the minimalist realized that the bowl had significant value both in money and sentiment. Minimalism can kill your heritage.

Homes are drowning in stuff. Most of you take in more and more and never find the opportunity to discard. Your homes fill up with duplicates and more stuff. You want to organize and keep everything. You purchase bigger containers and organization tips and tricks, but never organize stuff.

Organizing possessions is an action that needs to be taken all the time, and this is not a minimalist attitude. Balancing between minimalism and stuff is getting rid of stuff you no longer use so you can purchase things that will bring you happiness, be more useful, and bring more efficiency to your life.

Organizing is rearranging; remove excess stuff before purchasing more stuff. You can be an awesome consumer by following these few tips and tricks: If the stuff you have sitting on a shelf benefits no one, throw it away. Give it to friends who might use the item.   If you have stuff that does not solve debt problems; sell it. Don't build storage closets or shelters just to house your stuff; get rid of it. Organization does not prevent you from purchasing items that are duplicate items. Get rid of things you don't use.

While rearranging your stuff, you might want to evaluate why you have this stuff. Removing possessions from your home forces you to question the useful value of our stuff. Decide what possessions are truly most important and valuable to you. Organizing provides a temporary lift to attitudes. It clears rooms and cleans out your mind. Now throw away duplicates and pave the way for major lifestyle changes. Think about where you are going. Minimalism means decluttering. However, you should not let this philosophy turn your home into a monk's cell. There are tips and tricks to decluttering that will balance minimalism.

Organize first and buy second. It is not necessary to

go out and buy storage pieces and supplies when sorting through your home. Avoiding purchasing storage pieces; this combines both frugality and minimalism. You don't need those pretty boxes and bins if they don't fit the space you have. Hold what you need these storage containers to hold and make sure they function for your particular space. Clean out first, assess what you need and then purchase a few things. You can always add mores storage bins and items, but you don't want to purchase storage containers to clutter up your home.

Do not set aside the entire day to minimalize your home. No one has the energy or focus to spend all day organizing and decluttering. You will become frustrated and less efficient. Spend a few hours on one project or space. By working in small bites, you will not get burned out by the process. In addition, you will not throw away valuable times just to follow a minimalist philosophy.

Finish each decluttering task completely before moving on to something else. Once you have decided where something is going to go. In other words, never keep bags for charity or things to go to a friend in your home to deliver later. Do it right the first time. Take the bags and boxes out to the curb or recycling plant immediately. If you are donating things put the items in your car and make sure you deliver them the same day. Complete the deal or you will find yourself pulling stuff out of bags and boxes and keeping it.

Do not think once you have decluttered your space you are done. You have created a new and efficient system for processing and managing your stuff. Once you have decluttered, use the frugal approach and do not think about purchasing the same item again. Do regular clean up, but do not become obsessive compulsive. Avoid minimalist thinking that everything must go. Be practical and keep those items that you will need now and in the future. Avoid duplicates; that is the balance.

Be sensible. Your space will never look like those magazine pictures of awesome storage and decluttered places. If perfection is your goal, you will be disappointed. Your goal is to set up a space that works for you. Success is putting your hands on your hips at the end of the day and feeling satisfied with your work.

"Minimalism is the intentional promotion of the things we most value and the removal of everything that distracts us from it" (Becker, 2015). Don't let the term minimalist bring up images of destitution, small homes, barren walls, and no food in the cupboard. No stuff is not the way to enjoy life. Become rational and unfussy and keep the things, and the stuff, that is most valuable to you.

Look for a lifestyle that works for you. Use your imagination and find a style that is not cumbersome, but frees you based on your passions and desires. Your ultimate happiness does not depend on "less is more" or "keeping up with the Jones'." It is your attitude about what makes you secure, happy, and fulfilled.

Conclusion

"Choices are the hinges of destiny" ~ Pythagoras

There is a definite downside to minimalism. Everything has a cost, and everyone has needs, things that need to be done, duties and the need for stuff. Those that choose to keep only 100 possessions or less and give up their cars, phones, and homes are actually shifting their burdens to those around them. They are becoming more reliant on others instead of themselves. This seems to be counter to one of the rules of minimalism – take care of yourself.

The less stuff you have, the more likely you will have to borrow someone else's stuff. Now you are relying on someone else not be a minimalist so you can borrow what you need. You have to rely on others for rides to and from work.

A minimalist means you are dependent on others, and they expect something in return for their generosity. You promise to do something for them, but you don't since you are minimalist and forget what is going on. Being reliant on others is not simplification. It is stressful and frustrating on both parties. Keeping your possessions to a bare minimum makes it very unlikely that you will be prepared when disasters strike. Again, you are taking from others to serve your own needs.

It is not practical to cut yourselves off from the world by getting rid of technology or your cell phones and computers. Even people in third world countries have cell phones. If you use technology properly, you will keep your independence.

Severely limiting what you own makes it difficult to get anything done. You don't have the tools to work, you end up wasting time, and you are unproductive. The job doesn't get done properly. This is frustrating to you and on your friends and family.

You will never get others on board with a minimalistic lifestyle when they see how you live. You are constantly borrowing, being unreliable, and some-what self-centered. Being a minimalist is an uphill battle in today's image conscious world. Minimalism in its extreme form is not good for anyone. Take a more balanced approach to minimalism if you must. Minimalism should never be entered into without a great deal of thought. Minimalism can be good for you, and you may never regret following through with your decision.

Minimalism is a choice to live in a counter-cultural. Your life has revolved around the need to consume and collect. Now, once you have become a minimalist you reject those consuming and collecting messages and choose to live a simple life instead.   A minimalist lifestyle places experiences above stuff. It is, however, more than just throwing away clutter and organizing. It is a journey that takes part in your mind, soul, and heart. Choosing to be a minimalist will affect your entire world. Your emotions will need to be re-evaluated, and your values will be rocked. At its very core, minimalism in the intentional decluttering or putting aside the things you most value. It means for you to remove anything that detracts you from the valuable emotions, thoughts and experiences in your life. As you ponder becoming a minimalist, you may think that you have spent too much of your life pursuing things that are not all that valuable. You are now stressed because you have spent your entire life pursuing stuff. You begin to be plagued with "what ifs" and "whys". Minimalism can drive you crazy with these thoughts.

Minimalism denies the world that invents, produces, and promotes. Everyone loves their stuff. Stuff is security, who you are, and how you think about yourself. When your mindset has changed to simplify, society will be somewhat unforgiving. Culture looks much different when you get rid of stuff. You may think you will be happy and not regret your decisions to get rid of stuff. But people are creatures of habit, and acquiring stuff is what people do. You will soon regret that cell phone you tossed, your lack of furniture, and your old job, friends, and possibly some of your family.

Minimalists state that you will have more time, more freedom, more money, and much less stress. Your lifestyle will change. You will get out of debt, work less, travel more, and be one of the thousands of bloggers writing about minimalist. Really? How do you travel more without funds and stuff, how will you get out of debt without a job? Or the possibility of promotion? You simplify your life to the extent that you are not passionate about what you do; you go nowhere in your career.

Becoming a minimalist will cause you to be an anomaly. You will love telling people about your decision to radically simplify, and they will find you unattractive, different and weird. They will step back from you at neighborhood and friend parties, leave you out of their plans, and treat you as too unusual to be around.

You have removed the stuff in your life now it is time to simplify your commitments, your goals, your diet, and your relationships. The decision to become minimalist will affect your entire life.

Think about the real downsides of minimalism before you jump into the fray:

Craigslist, eBay, and Goodwill are you friends. They own more of your stuff than you do.

No longer do you browse shopping sites and you

have no reason to go shopping. Now, what do you do with your spare time?

You might have enough money to travel so you grab your carry-on. As you enter customs, officers are a bit suspicious that you are really staying in their country for a month or more. This is a true scenario. A minimalist couple traveling overseas was stopped by customs for having too little luggage for their intended stay.

You friends will continually tease you since you only have two shirts. You are a joke among your friends and acquaintances.

No one asks you to go on road trips, to bars or out to dinner anymore. They know you will not offer to pay. You will expect everyone else to pay for you.   You sneak into malls and are very afraid that your acquaintances will see you and judge you as a hypocrite.

You don't have a television, and now you have to find other things to do. You can read or exercise. You will miss out on all the latest trends in fashion, food, and fun.

You don't buy gifts for the family or your friends anymore. The real downside, you don't get gifts either.

You will be accused of being trendy. People will wonder what a minimalist is and why you would want to be one.   Your clothes become frayed and faded. You are no longer welcome in good restaurants or at parties with friends.

When you have visitors, you get antsy about all the stuff they are bringing into your home. You want them to leave, and you get cranky and irritable. When you visit other people's homes, you mentally start clearing out their rooms.   If you have children, there is no way you are a minimalist.   People will feel threatened by you. They believe you are criticizing them for their materialistic lifestyle. You friends no longer show you their new technology and heaven forbid if you find out they have purchased a new car.

You don't have a car. You can no longer do your

share of giving rides and helping out when others are stranded. Also, people will think you are poor and jobless. If you are continually asking for rides, your friends and family will soon tell you to take the bus. To be or not to be a minimalist. That is the question. Minimalism is very difficult to define precisely. If you believe minimalism is defined by cutting back, consuming less, and being more thoughtful in regards to value, it is a great premise.

Materialism or holding on to stuff is also important. Ignore the definition that materialism has a tendency to worship material possessions and physical comfort more than spiritual values. Not so! People enjoy their comforts. It his were not so would you strive to live in a nice home, have awesome stuff around you, and snuggle up in a fuzzy blanket when you need comfort? There is nothing that says you can't be materialistic and spiritual at the same time. Take the example listed before, "There is nothing wrong with having and holding possessions. The Bible is full of stories of those who own much. How do minimalists reconcile God's riches with a desire to live a minimalist lifestyle? "God's home, the Temple, was adorned with gold beyond imagination" (Ps50:10). Do take a long and hard look at your life. You can cut back in places that don't really matter. You can be intentional, but avoid getting rid of all your stuff just to be "trendy". Live a simpler life, but keep what is important to you even if you crowd your space a bit with stuff.   It is true that most consumers do have way too much stuff, and much more than we need. It is an awesome thought to simplify. Stand back and examine what you can do without and where you can cut back. Balance minimalist with practicality. Be sensible in what you try to do without.   Think consciously about what you are doing when contemplating minimalism. Think about how you will spend your time. Minimalizing is pretty terrifying when you are trying to get exactly where you want to be. It is much easier to fill your life with distractions. Balance your stuff with experiences, memories, and value. Take a good hard look at where you are going with your lifestyle and be happy with who you are.